TOUCHED BY STARS

poems by

Margaret A. Fox

Finishing Line Press
Georgetown, Kentucky

TOUCHED BY STARS

Copyright © 2019 by Margaret A. Fox
ISBN 978-1-63534-837-8 First Edition
All rights reserved under International and Pan-American Copyright Conventions. No part of this book may be reproduced in any manner whatsoever without written permission from the publisher, except in the case of brief quotations embodied in critical articles and reviews.

ACKNOWLEDGMENTS

My gratitude to Susanne Fest, EdD, former Graduate School Chair of the Social Science Department at Antioch University Midwest, for her guidance and encouragement. Also, thank you to my learning and thesis mentor at Antioch University, Guy Burneko, PhD, for introducing me to cosmology and sustainability. In addition, I thank Brooke Crowley, PhD, professor in Geology and Anthropology at the University of Cincinnati, for coaching my exploration of the relationships between life on earth and the natural environment and asking me to render stories of hope. A thank you to Tracy Connor, who founded Tongue & Groove Midwest, and Nancy Neihaus, owner of The Clifton House, who hosts it. Also, I thank authors Kay Sloan, PhD, for encouraging me to do more writing and for her earlier edits, Patricia Henley, MFA, who advised me during the later stages of writing these poems, and Margaret Reich who did the proofing.

Publisher: Leah Maines
Editor: Christen Kincaid
Cover Art: Margaret A. Fox, *Fall Reflection*
Author Photo: Jason Sheldon
Cover Design: Christen Kincaid

Printed in the USA on acid-free paper.
Order online: www.finishinglinepress.com
        also available on amazon.com

        Author inquiries and mail orders:
        Finishing Line Press
        P. O. Box 1626
        Georgetown, Kentucky 40324
        U. S. A.

Table of Contents

Worthmore 1

Ecology of Love 3

First Steps 4

Infinity Scarf 6

Stardust 7

The Night Light 8

For the Time Being 9

Emanations 10

At One 11

Everyday Moments Over Time 12

Evolving in Uncertainty 13

A Part in Search of a Whole 14

Refugee 15

War Torn Phoenix 16

Calcutta Saint 17

Srinivasa Ramanujan 18

Melting 19

Rachel 20

Cosmology of a Tree 21

March 20th 22

Eclipse at The Littlefield 23

Worthmore

At noon church bells rang.
Children on the playground bowed their heads
recited *The Angelus*. An angel called, Mary responded.
The little girl walked home for lunch.

Awkward on the playground, she never
knew what to say. She lost her voice. *And blessed
is the fruit of thy womb.* She felt
a disconnection inside out.

Walk home lunches were quiet,
unlike evenings or weekends, the shouting stopped.
The pain lifted, memories faded. She ate her favorite soup,
Worthmore Turtle Soup, counted on it to fill the void.

Springtime in the woods,
filled the creek with crayfish. She caught them
then returned them. Lightening bugs
appeared in June. She pursued them as if catching stars.

Nature comforted her,
like the angel and Mary, her love for art
when she copied words for the postcard paintings
pasted in her notebook at school.

In nature, painting, or writing
space expanded, she emerged—fell silent
before Vincent's stars, at the Louvre
breathed in Leonardo's final painting.

Fra Angelico's *Annunciation* in Florence,
All made the postcard paintings alive again,
as did Millet's *Angelus*-
life *dwelt* in her.

When she hiked, heard a bird,
walked alongside the ocean, listening to ancient voices
where life began, she remembered – Worthmore,
what it meant to be brought back to life.

A woman *graced*,
her fiat to a world full of dichotomies
created in the name of love made flesh.
Her body made whole again on Earth.

Ecology of Love

We dined alfresco. The only ones seated,
gazing at a full moon, plus stars Venus and Mars.
Venus the ruling planet, feeling the tension of Mars.

The waitress assumed we were lovers.
Dark, I asked for a candle, she brought two.
Both embarrassed, what could not be acknowledged may be seen.

Contemplatives express in silence
what it takes to transform energies of one into another,
make it better, capable of love, to create.

The Confucian sage assists bringing Heaven and Earth together,
a triad, ruled by a purity of heart, precepts,
what it takes to nurture and sustain creation.

Even as creation grows as it groans,
the sage comprehends all ten thousand things,
Earth's abundance for human flourishing.

We give birth to scientific discoveries, myths,
children, meaning of life conversations,
poetry, love, forgiveness.

You, me, us expanding in the universe,
eating, gazing, loving silently.
Under a full moon, we watched two stars.

First Steps

Stepping out first,
    man, woman, and child from East Africa.
Uncertain, curious, one hundred fifty of five thousand,
    two-footed people – why travel so far?

They experienced how they knew
    what they knew.
What to do with understanding, bifurcation
    to survive, interactions that changed them.

Relating they-thou both evolved,
    a mutual ongoing getting to know you.
Women gave birth with less time to gather,
    Men gathered then hunted.

Their hands took shape as learning tools,
    they grasped then let go.
Painted their stories on cave walls,
    at Altimira in Spain, in France …

I painted on canvas deconstructing natural images,
    to know what I knew.
My hands grasp a brush, theirs charcoal sticks,
    I purchase colors, they made them.

Fonte-de-Gaum, chromatic cave paintings,
    Cave painters shaped reindeer.
Images that bowed to the other, initial signs
    of deer affection grew later too dear.

Peche Merle, Lot Valley,
   I imagined painting with them,
Touching the curved stone cave walls,
    the curve that merged into a bison's back—a triumphant l'oeil.

Men, women, children,
   over millions of years,
Brought forth a world, touched by
   a constant dynamic knowing.

Infinity Scarf

The woman shopped for an infinity scarf. An oval shaped material
that could orbit around her neck. She took her time to find that one scarf
to express a particle or element she carried inside her.
She wanted to share it, communicate with it. Get to know it better.

She spotted a multi-colored scarf. Deep blues burst into purple shifted
to violet with a burst of white. Quasars scattered throughout the pattern.
She rotated the scarf around her neck. Looked in the mirror astonished.
Shoppers turned their heads, hands shielded eyes toward a light.

Seeing her reflection, she could no longer contain her energy.
The patterned scarf turned into the Milky Way Galaxy. She had
wrapped the Milky Way Galaxy around her neck. Like a star
in the universe, sheer joy and energy expanded in her.

She thought she would burst.
Sprinting over to her sister—"Look I'm a star in the universe."
Her sister looked and knew, what she always knew—
"That scarf is you."

All the other elements of the stars, making up part of the universe,
shopping that evening, continued to rotate around each other.
They traveled through an expanding universe on earth.
Most, unknowingly, comforted by Copernicus.

When they awoke the next morning,
the sun remained at the center of the universe
stunning them all with a brilliant energy
of belonging, a *cosmogenesis*.

Stardust

Flecks of stardust fell on their shoulders,
the people soon twinkled.
They truly sparkled, then
a child softly began to sing.

"Twinkle, twinkle little stars,
how I wonder what we are.
It makes me happy to know I'm a star,
connecting to all of you who are."

Slowly as the child continued to sing,
something began to lift all the stars on Earth.
Lift them up into the sky just in time for night,
what a sight, their constellating at night.

Seeing they believed, the energy that lifted,
clearly touched them all and gifted
Those who related on ground to the universe so high.
Why, oh why, did it take so long to fly?

The Night Light

They looked up from the beginning of their time on Earth,
  held captive by the luminosity in the night time sky.
As men, women and children, they wondered,
  who made these lights in the sky?
Perhaps some energy or magic tried to talk,
  the way they talked when painting bison, horses, or bears in caves.
They looked up from the beginning of their time on Earth. Astonished-
  night time lights appeared, disappeared and reappeared.
The light Einstein would bend, and Planck would call quantum,
  light appearing everywhere.
A mysterious light hidden in the men, women and children,
  who wondered, and found comfort in knowing
That they did not know. They went on wondering
  why and how and from where this light shone.
A compass that gave them direction
  at night and discovery by day.

For the Time Being

Sometimes it is before spring that seeds are planted,
    Just as your DNA reveals in time some of what will be.
Tiny shoots appear out of the dark moist ground,
    Almost like a question you asked me at the beginning.
A ground of being filled with bacteria and nutrients all at the same time,
    What will become of us?
Crocus, daffodils, baby leaves poking through some stormy weather,
    What will be, become, of us, as we grow and emerge
    as self and selves together?
It will be so after the storm, what is concealed will be revealed slowly,
    Beauty, weakness, strength, may be nonlinear appearances
    of life unfolding.
Moment making creations of how goes it in the world,
    A world of quiet moments, being-blossoms, ready to open.

Emanations

Holst composed a whole symphony about The Planets,
  spinning around the sun, each with its own rhythm and motif.
Blake, a poem to shed light, meaning between a Lamb and *Tyger*
  burning bright, to acknowledge contrast and human awareness
  in being and livelihood on Earth.

Bursting forth from the tension of dark energy and matter,
  yet here we are in a galaxy that pulls us in and together by sheer gravity.
An electromagnetic field through the speed of curved light,
  a non-local event that causes all of us to live in and outside
  of one another.

A family reunion of sorts whose tree grows as its place and space expands,
  from darkness insisting on its companion light, so stars relate
  to life on Earth.
Life, whose roots grow deeper from East Africa to North America,
  small bands of humans exploring to survive, raw in their inventiveness.

Is it any wonder that we wandered as stardust from the beginning of time?
  Empty nesters again, only to realize another part of their whole.
Is it any wonder that we saw stories in light patterns – cosmologies colliding
  with spiritual beliefs, dualism, not knowing yet what truly is sacred.

At One

The light came in as she meditated,
A brilliant opening occurred.
She motioned to it with her attention,
awareness entered.
Just sitting, not doing, breathing, waiting with attention,
she pulled her breath up from the ground to the top of her head
and beyond.
The breath returned uninterrupted, from above her head and down again,
a cylindrical motion of energy that grew as she did internally.
Her body position sprouted roots deep in the Earth and above in the Sky,
Suddenly her breath reached the stars, changed to a brilliant white light.
Down came the light again, going from head to toe, and back,
Pure white light moved, from a starry night, to dusk, to day, to night.
She felt herself on a mountain precipice of imagination and knowing,
A space where she could see everything at the same time.
Yet, everything was not in motion, only in relationship,
appearing as a warmth in the belly of her being, all while sitting still.

Everyday Moments over Time

We become something different over time
  by circumstance, choice, or necessity.
Swearing not to repeat, yet we do.
  Then in one poignant moment we see, hear, understand.
Expansion comes at a price or not or somewhere in between-
  relying on circumstance, choice, necessary moments. We search
for love, find it, lose it, return it, maybe
  over time begin to notice what it takes.
Every moment the universe expands beyond our grasp
  we bow, fall to our knees, wail in front of a wall,
Pilgrimage, walk into a river,
  to love, honor, obey, be set free—relate to something bigger.

Evolving in Uncertainty

Between bonobo and chimpanzee, human primates evolved,
  an enactment of coupling.
Apes and humans shared DNA, four-legged to two-legged,
  a natural drift into humanity.
A bunch of two-leggeds,
  on the way to being in one world.
Unsure, act on certainties that change daily,
  search for what remains in flux.
Grasp at post dandelion seeds floating in the air,
  discover, deconstruct, desire.
Live life in moments.

A Part in Search of a Whole

A self, a part made whole again.
Wants to know, reason, feel another,
cells of life on Earth.
Object becomes subject, subject becomes object,
one living organism.
A request, petition, demand for *poiesis*,
to make, an eco-peace be or go with you.
Life on Earth, parts reflecting each other,
become a whole new effect.
Observation, insight make a discovery embraceable.
Embodiment beckons the sum of its parts
to understand a mystery, a path
made up of energies,
a poet begging for alms to make us live again.

Refugee

Leonard Cohen says "we'll come to love like a refugee"
born out of a war-torn land bearing a heart needing care.
The borders of our love challenged by trust,
Takes a toll on those who risk coming and those who welcome.

A broken trust blows up limbs, divides families, breaks hearts,
for what—*Et pluribus unum?*
Trust offered from another's eyes, words, touch and concern,
cause one to do it all over again, begging for a different outcome.

Enslaved once, humans seize opportunity, shake off shackles
of greed, prison, the fundamentalism in all beliefs.
You sought refuge, trusted in me, counted on us,
to live and love in a land created by a desire to be free.

War Torn Phoenix

A Syrian freedom fighter
  Reached into the rubble, pulled out a crying infant.
Soldiers cheered—
  a child reborn out of war, love and freedom.
The news told the story,
  behold a miracle, honor, cherish it.
Two weeks pass,
  the soldier died.
War exacts a price from existential us—
  fear, a lie, told in love's absence.

Calcutta Saint

She stirred the hearts of millions,
Tending to the dying in the streets.
The lowliest of the low,
untouchables to most of us.

Acknowledged by the world,
due to acting on what could not be done.
Caring without expectation
a return of a life time of deeds well done.

After her death sainthood
seemed in keeping with her self-sacrifice.
What was required
To become the Saint Calcutta Nun?

A witness came forth,
said thinking about the would-be saint
Caused inexplicable change in her life.
The first proof of sainthood.

What was convincing, not *Curia* conniving,
came through letters to her confessor.
Descriptions of her suffering
caused by taking on the walking-on-water man's being.

No separation between her and him,
full integration belief and practice,
caused a lifetime of depression,
begged the question how to get out of Gethsemane?

The Calcutta saint knew pain.
Did she know joy?
Recipients of her love knew joy in their pain,
if only for a brief time.

A sinner nun who walked on water,
a beyond in-the-line-of-duty original blessing.
A complex evolutionary, a transformation
flowing from I, to you, in me, to us.

Srinivasa Ramanujan

You counted on infinity
through the Hindu goddess, Lakshmi.
Your goddess of good fortune
looked over your village in India.
You meditated, paid homage to her.
She responded with prime numbers.
They spiraled down, you went up to meet them.
You met her and others.
Expansion led you to Cambridge.
Good fortune followed
with your G. H. Hardy teacher.
You worked backwards from the divine to the human.
From the answer you shaped the theory,
searching for the origins of the universe.
You a star became the first brown
Fellow Royal Academy of Science.
Hardy believed in you.
Lakshmi always believed in you,
led you to infinity,
only to find the beginning.

Melting

Can you hear it? Glaciers melting.
The sound will make or break us,
First felt by below sea level coastal areas, set in motion
by below sea level monsters of greed and development.

19th through 21st Centuries style, fossil fueling the world.
If only the fossil-like thinking in high and low places could realize,
we are not fossils, but real—breathing, feeling, life giving
creatures who can vote.

We know. We see.
Thank you, James Balog,
polar express picture-taking explorer of ice,
glaciers in all their glorious colors of white, gray, blue and green.

Your pics captured the melt down.
Now we can see and feel the problem,
A frozen reflection of the ocean,
the melt down again and again.

Now picture a prehistoric, historic and present melt,
the glacier melt moved in 10 years what it once did in 100.
It made you cry … and cry … and cry, and
fight through tears for your daughters' future, and more to come.

Rachel

It's another silent spring.
Why did you wait until the end to say there is a way out?
Industry dumped, poisoned knowingly.
Farmers sprayed DDT, government approved it.
The early bird caught the night crawling worm.
Poison passed from worms to robins—
dead on arrival, Michigan State campus.
Remember as a child the robin sang the song of spring.
Now hope springs eternal in silence.
Still, quiet, subtle, lasting, goes on forever.
Shakespeare would say *Love's Labor Lost* …
or *to Be or Not to Be… Boil, Boil, Toil and Trouble*
… *Something's rotten in Denmark.*
If that's true, and we know it's all true.
Don't repeal Rachel's act that protects
what holds wonder, runs wild and pure,
quenches our thirst, keeps us warm
without making people go hungry,
or worse, go to war.

Cosmology of a Tree

What grows here may grow there. Go into the forest.
Let me know what you see. Are you asking for a survey?
No, the outcome of a creation story, post apple, Adam and Eve.
What it means to live ashamed of nakedness, covered up ... separate
from nature ... a mystery ... a tree growing in Brooklyn.

In the beginning, Japanese scientist, Miki, finds a tree fossil in 1940,
names it *Metasequoia*, WWII breaks out, loss of many lives and loves,
caused by a short mean mustached man. He and followers decimated
a people of Old Testament cosmology, Hebrews,
and New Testament people too.

Peace arrives. Welcomed! A message sent
from Japan to China. Several years pass.
Cheng and Hu confirm a new discovery, *Metasequoia*.
From this ancient tree, during peace, seeds were retrieved.
Spread throughout the world, to places whose earth was moist.

The discovered ancient tree grows tall near water ... now.
Across the world, a *Red Dawn* rises, a *Metasequoia*,
planted at daybreak in Brooklyn.
Urban reforestation, a re-creation story, a natural forest cover,
I pull it over my naked body at night saying thank you.

March 20th

I made soup—
potatoes, leeks, onions, butter, wine
with a dash of Himalayan pink salt.
A recipe for a fine
flash lightening, raining day.
I played favorite tunes,
cooked, danced in the kitchen.
Stirred the pot, whirled to the music,
like a half-crazed Sufi praising the universe.
I paused, tasted the rainy-day creation,
Wondered if all of it was a necessary ingredient,
to fall in love with myself again.

Eclipse at The Littlefield

The moon travelled diagonally,
Washington to the South Carolina shore.
Dazed, I look up through shaded spectacles—
Watched the most anticipated viewing
in ninety-nine years.
Sun partners with the moon,
trades places, waxing and waning,
from light to dark to light again.
Do we reflect the same movement?
Oh Moon, you call the oceanic tides,
the water in my body responds,
changing my thoughts and feelings.
Sipping my Solar Eclipse drink outside,
I watch and wait for the arrival of total darkness,
inching towards light. I hear a wow from voices,
murmuring among the lush plantings on the patio.
A waiter taps my shoulder,
points to the stone patio.
Shadows of sun crescent patterns shimmer,
by the breath of a breeze.

Margaret A. Fox has performed in the New Jersey Opera Festival, The Street Theater of Princeton, NJ, and most recently as a poet at Tongue & Groove Midwest in Cincinnati, Ohio. She received the Mayor of the City of Cincinnati Humanitarian Award in 2016 for her work on local immigration reform, as the executive director of the Metropolitan Area Religious Coalition of Cincinnati, an interfaith nonprofit that seeks local resolution of social justice concerns through public policy.

www.ingramcontent.com/pod-product-compliance
Lightning Source LLC
LaVergne TN
LVHW041522070426
835507LV00012B/1761